Princeton Architectural Press/New York

CW00740228

james   frank   terence
cathcart, fantauzzi, van elslander

pamphlet architecture 25

gravity

Published by
Princeton Architectural Press
37 East Seventh Street
New York, New York 10003

For a free catalog of books, call
1.800.722.6657.
Visit our web site at www.papress.com.

©2003 Princeton Architectural Press
All rights reserved
Printed and bound in the United States
11 10 09 5 4 3 2

This project is supported in part by an award from the National Endowment for the Arts.

No part of this book may be used or reproduced in any manner without written permission from the publisher, except in the context of reviews.

Every reasonable attempt has been made to identify owners of copyright. Errors or omissions will be corrected in subsequent editions.

Editor: Linda Lee
Designer: James Cathcart with Nancy C. Hoerner

Special thanks to: Nettie Aljian, Nicola Bednarek, Janet Behning, Megan Carey, Penny (Yuen Pik) Chu, Russell Fernandez, Jan Haux, Clare Jacobson, Mark Lamster, Nancy Eklund Later, Nancy Levinson, Katharine Myers, Jane Sheinman, Scott Tennent, Jennifer Thompson, Joe Weston, and Deb Wood of Princeton Architectural Press—Kevin C. Lippert, publisher

Library of Congress
Cataloging-in-Publication Data

Cathcart, James, 1962–

Gravity / James Cathcart, Frank Fantauzzi, Terence Van Elslander.—1st ed.
p. cm. — (Pamphlet architecture ; 25)

ISBN 1-56898-434-0 (pbk.)

1. Communication in architectural design—United States. 2. Group work in architecture—United States. 3. Conceptual art—Influence. I. Fantauzzi, Frank, 1957– II. Van Elslander, Terence, 1957– III. Title. IV. Series.

NA2750 .C38 2003
720'.973'09045—dc21

2003011259

Pamphlet Architecture was initiated in 1977 as an independent vehicle to criticize, question, and exchange views. Each issue is assembled by an individual author/architect. For more information, pamphlet proposals, or contributions please write to Pamphlet Architecture, c/o Princeton Architectural Press, 37 East Seventh Street, New York, New York, 10003.

Pamphlets published:

*Out of print. Available only in the collection *Pamphlet Architecture 1–10.*

table of contents

Foreword

Cathcart, Fantauzzi, Van Elslander

"An object on the wall does not confront gravity: it timidly resists it … the ground plane, not the wall, is the necessary support for the maximum awareness of the object."

—Robert Morris

It's simple.

Our motivation springs from curiosity: to see, to understand, and to act. Episodically for fifteen years, we have met, talked, and made. The context of our meetings drives the work. Material is found, sometimes existing in the situation itself, or chosen practically. The work resolves over time by the doing of it. When we discuss our work, we describe the experience of it: how it is made, how it works, how it feels. The final product is not important. We can change our minds. The specifics of and the relationship between situation and material are what we discuss.

Our work is like a lever: it opens, measures, illuminates, but also creates a connection. It weighs a moment against a place, an event against an object. It finds a crack and widens it.

We make functions.

Constructing Essences

Juhani Pallasmaa

"Destroying and constructing are equal in importance, and we must have souls for the one and the other," argues Phaedrus to his friend Socrates in Paul Valéry's *Eupalinos,* or *The Architect,* in their dialogue on the essence of architecture.[1] These seemingly opposite acts are equal in the sense that they are both ways of altering existing reality. Construction always implies destruction of a prior state of being, changing and rearranging physical, cultural, and experiential conditions. Both processes reveal and hide; they release possibilities or disguise what has been. Architecture transforms the world through the projection of distinct intentionality, purpose, and meaning.

Understanding construction as a mere visual formalism annuls the essence of the fundamental human act of building. The meaning of architecture is not in its aesthetics, but in the transformation of infinite and meaningless space into a specific place of action, signification, and symbolization, providing limitless and measureless physical time with a human experiential measure. We inhabit the world through acts of architecture.

Architecture frames and scales, re-directs and focuses, re-defines and re-names, connects and disconnects, re-balances and re-orients. Every act of construction has its unconscious motives and reflects a metaphysical position— a specific understanding of the self and the world.

Buildings are inhabited metaphors, which simultaneously change and preserve, domesticate and alienate, protect and terrify. As the French philosopher Maurice Merleau-Ponty suggests, we live in the flesh of the world. Dwelling in this flesh implies an intertwining and exchange: we exist in the world, and the world exists in us. Consequently, as we build, we also transform our corporeal and mental constitutions. We know who we are and where we come from primarily through the slow accumulation of architectural structures. History is a constructed artifact. Architecture concretizes and reinforces the very history of culture and individual life. Phaedrus confesses to Socrates, "I truly believe that I have constructed myself," and thereby rejects the view of self as a given.[2]

Domestic fly density at third floor, elevation twenty-eight feet above street level

Architecture is usually understood as a construction of beauty, but the essence of architecture is not in its visual form or gestalt. The phenomenon of architecture cannot even be properly named, because it does not have a noun essence. It is nameless;, it is a verb, an event. Rather than an object, architecture is a confrontation, interaction, and exchange. It lends us its authority and aura, whereas we, on our behalf, give architecture its mental and emotive power. The submerged and liquid imagery of Michelangelo's stair hall in the Bibliotheca Laurentiana, for instance, does not make me melancholic through its forms and appearances; the architectural work allures feelings of melancholy from my very soul, and it reflects them back to me through my senses. The architectural work makes me confront my own *melancholia*.

The architectural works of Cathcart, Fantauzzi, and Van Elslander reject the idea of architecture as a predefined discipline or a category of given purpose. These projects are simultaneously artistic and architectural propositions, philosophical investigations and metaphysical assumptions, excavations and constructions, archaeology and invention, rationality and absurdity. They reveal the mental significance of construction by questioning, subordinating, or eliminating utilitarian purpose. The meaning is found, discovered, and identified, rather than projected. The methodology of these explorations bypasses the notion of aesthetics: beauty resides in the very act of discovery, rather than in the externalized object. Aesthetics is transformed into material and embodied processes of making. These projects explore and valorize the mental essences of architecture through physical encounters and confrontations. The idea is carried through with ritualistic fervor and mesmerizing repetition and perseverance. As Socrates states: "The greatest liberty is born of the greatest rigor."[3] Thought and matter, idea and execution, inspiration and end result, become inseparable. Thought turns into existence, discipline into freedom and discovery.

[1] Paul Valéry, *Dialogues*, Bollingen Series XLV (New York: Pantheon Books, 1956), 70.
[2] Ibid., 81.
[3] Ibid., 131.

Density at basement, elevation six feet below street level

Cranbrook Academy of Art, Bloomfield Hills, Michigan, 1989

A gallery space was divided in half by cutting and rotating a portion of the ceiling vertically.

Rotation process

University at Buffalo, Buffalo, New York, 1999

A 35' x 5' portion of wall was cut and rotated about a verticle axis to reconnect two spaces that were once continuous.

Not-P

Kent Kleinman

The body of work of Cathcart, Fantauzzi, and Van Elslander should not be discussed in terms of process versus product, building versus drawing, operation versus form, Gordon Matta-Clark, installation art, Richard Serra's verb list, traces, or site-specific sculpture—temptation to the contrary notwithstanding. For to do so is to situate the work at arms length from a host of normative forces that are at once responsible for the shape of the built environment and responsible for the shape of many of the projects depicted here.

Cutting process

Take, for example, the project *Slice*. The 35' x 5' wall section, rotated ninety degrees, violated a rated fire wall separating two spaces: the remaining wall fragment was not sufficiently high to serve as a guardrail for protecting viewers from the twelve-foot drop to the lower gallery. The construction work was done with illicit labor, with minimal drawings, which consisted mostly of ad hoc sketches, augmented with verbal commands. The exoskeleton trusses that held the wall fragment together, while engineered, were never subjected to code review. No building inspectors visited the site during construction. There was no budget agreement, no contract, and no legal framework for the project. Under the guise of impermanence, myriad regulatory parameters were skirted. The site was part gallery, part abandoned attic space, environments that camouflaged the ongoing work.

These bureaucratic infractions are, in the context of conventional practice, not negligible. They are precisely the parameters that make this project "not possible." These infractions are not marginal consequences of the project; they are central to the work's critical agenda. This is not to deny that the corpus exudes a poetic sensibility or that it has the potential to arouse an attitude of aesthetic distraction. But if the work is poetic, it is also critical; the two are not the same, nor are they necessarily related. The criticality of the work, arousing the opposite reaction to distraction, lies in exposing what the institutional, regulatory, and cultural environment, the horizon of the architectural imagination, occludes. There is a method employed that amounts to a strategy.

The first step of this strategy is the complete elimination of drawings. This is not the result of a preference for other projective modalities, such as models and animations, for there are essentially no a priori representations at all. Thus, there are no means for articulating, judging, predicting, or composing in advance of building. Drawings, together with specifications, divide and direct labor. The only precise specifications of the projects included in this volume are statistics compiled after the work was executed (i.e., "one hundred gallons of latex," "forty-six hundred palettes," "twenty thousand shoes," and so on).

The inversion/perversion of function is the second step. The means-end rationality of the world is delayed, linearity becomes circular (*Car Spin*), and habitation destroys dwelling (imagine trying to actually inhabit the space opened by the *Push/Pull* project). The third step involves challenging our distracted consumption of the built environment with work that reintroduces risk, if not danger, into a neutralized and standardized world. This corpus has teeth, which is the fourth critical move. There is no polish, no finishing in the traditional sense of the detail, but rather cutting without sutures. There is recycling unburdened by actual reuse (*Big Orbits*) and diagnosis unconcerned with rehabilitation (*Editing Detroit*). Finally, there is special treatment reserved for the photographic image, which serves here as witness. The "crime-scene" or "surveillance-camera" mode of photography dominates this volume: there is almost no gloss, and backgrounds are almost always cluttered. We catch the work, fleetingly, becoming itself. The work's impermanence, rather than architecture's traditional durability, is anticipated and documented in the images. It is not quite true that there are no representations; they simply come at the end rather than the beginning of the building process.

As the list above suggests, the works are intricately bound to conventions. It is a dependent relationship. A serious alternative practice develops a coherence proportional to that which it opposes. Herein lies at least one cause for the work's rigor: it is not free. It is a response to a perceived lack rather than an act of imagination ex nihilo. Its territory is already prepared, its site already determined by prior architectural acts. The pit for the buried van in *Excavation*, for example, is precisely the extent of the existing parking spot painted on the asphalt surface; this demarcation, the received site of action, was predrawn. Similarly, the position of the body of the truck above grade was predetermined by the physiognomy of the vehicle: inverted and repositioned, the tops of the tires (normally the bottom) precisely touch grade (the top of the concrete cast). The project team simply (well, not simply) inverted the found condition.

Limits and lineaments set by preceding practices are essential to much of the work. This is why the preferred sites are always congested, always preinhabited, never virgin, never unbuilt. Even the extraordinary labor invested in the work is predetermined, for it bears a distinct and respectful relationship to the investment required to construct the found condition. The labor of unbuilding a house is balanced against building one, casting and dismantling a truck balanced against stamping and assembling one; repositioning a wall and a ceiling is balanced against the original act of erecting a stable wall and a horizontal ceiling.

In a recent text titled *Excluded Middle: Toward a Reflective Architecture and Urbanism*, architectural theorist Edward Dimendberg argues for a mode of practice situated in what he terms the "excluded middle."[1] The excluded middle is a product of Aristotelian logic wherein a subject cannot be both a predicate and its negation. P or not-P, either black or not-black, either cat or not-cat: the middle term, *both black and not-black*, is logically excluded. However, Dimendberg suggests that an appropriate practice for a time characterized by contradictory valuations and competing technologies should be of the "both/and" type, a middle position that enthusiastically enters the contemporary fray by recognizing and celebrating our fundamentally multivalent cultural and technological conditions. I have periodically pondered the possibility of understanding the work here as inhabiting such a middle ground or if not actually inhabiting it, then being sufficiently close to be nudged into that territory. I now believe that the work does not function in this way. The work is oppositional in a binary manner that does not desire synthesis or embody a third term. It is not a model or a demonstration of excluded possibilities. It is, pace Dimendberg, more important than that. It is an example of the *not-possible*, without which no middle term is imaginable.

[1] Edward Dimendberg, *Excluded Middle: Toward a Reflective Architecture and Urbanism* (Houston and San Francisco: Rice School of Architecture and William Stout Publishers, 2002), 22.

View from gallery

View from reclaimed space

Columbus, Ohio, 1993
With Tim Mizicko, Sean Murphy, Will Stanforth, Joseph Plenzler

The drivetrain of a Toyota Corolla was reconfigured
to spin the car around a point.

Reconfigured drivetrain

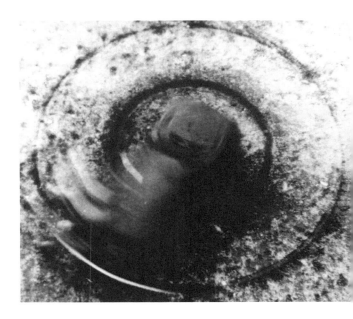

Tar on Sheetrock, 1988

Willis Art Gallery, Detroit, Michigan, 1989

With Jean-Claude Azar and Michael Williams

A typical working-class house in a decayed neighborhood was purchased and disassembled by hand. The house had been abandoned with all of the occupants' possessions. The parts of the house were indexed by material for public display: wood siding, two-by-fours, lath, plaster, shingles, metal ducts, wire, nails, and ashes.

At the end of the display, all of the elements of the entire house fit into a single thirty-five-cubic-yard commercial dumpster.

Site 1989

Site 1990

Day 1

Day 3

9119 St. Cyril

Harah Frost

Called upon to feel and not to think, I watched a process evolve from devolution. "And on the eighth day they took it down." A kind of internship in reverse for five architects. The backdrop was the winter. Though sunny, the days were bitter cold. There was no utopia here, no "green world" process of discovery or transformation wrought by taking time out from paid labors and identifiable reasons. No carneval, or else a dark one.

The third in a row of wrecks, this house is an item strewn. The plaster is darkened, chipped, and coming away, the basement full of drug paraphernalia and spent shells. Because a hole in the roof in the kitchen caused the ceiling to ice over, the elements are evident inside, no longer commanded. After outside and inside are confused, what other contradictions appear? What could this opened house hold? It was an unpleasant place that one found to be pleasant, breathing blue of plaster, lines of lath. It held an irrationality that haunted and permitted, a cold that was both bone deep and purging, an anxiety that provoked curses but also tenderness like bruised skin. One was always wondering, coming back to a question, touching it. It held a labor that was both meaningless and engaging, since intense focus on the task is as true for making as unmaking. I watched the architect circle the perimeter, assess the before and after, the up and down, the composed and de-composed, re-align nails and sills with hammer and crowbar, lay bare sockets, take an ax to a once polished floor.

Standing by, I make the analogy between self and house, asking: could you take me apart, pommel and dis-articulate, reduce from complex to simple by following diagrams done to undone? When do you take the inside walls down? The reasons will echo. Which are the crucial studs? Inside uprights are a forest. Which walls are extra, peripheral? How do you find out? Is the house a cross or a square, and is there some beam holding the idea, atlaslike? If one misunderstood crux and periphery, who would get hurt?

Say the square box of outside walls define a space you thought you knew. If you take one away and are left with three, you have a theater, and inside are merely players, not people. If you infinitely radiate the lines left by two perpendicular walls, you embrace everything south by southwest. Extrapolate from the line left by one wall and you have a wavering commitment. It is down now, unsightly shell removed, innards voided, danger passed, question closed. At ground level, the project refused to fetishize, left no evocative fragment.

Day 5

A writer facing her habits of construction was disconcerted, looking for the coherent point to make or position to take. The "anxious observer" suited the time and place. For relief, I invented an intercessor. I found a name on a letter in the basement, Rhonda, that I took to be the last tenant, so I wondered about her. Could she answer questions about why this was being done? Did she see things differently after it was over? Did I? But if, of all things possible, she would walk down that silent, vaguely sunny, winter street, and stop to chat, I would ask, How did these architects come to assume the landscape was there to be used? If the site looked like a hole in the neighborhood to them, what did it look like to someone trained differently? Was the architect's relationship to the neighborhood antagonistic? Perplexed? At what level is the project exploitive? Incomprehensible? What could they have done that would have been an addition to the area and not a subtraction? Was it easy to get a permit? Why? Does the concept of gallery (where debris landed) legitimize by generalizing the object, that is, house and beam? Is Platonic purity found in the depths of Detroit? Where does my complicity in the idealization begin when I find the thing so beautiful? What is lost in cutting away the real? Especially, what metaphors made this project possible?

Day 6

The work could mean nothing. The walls could mean nothing. It is making me nervous that it sits, a body *morcele,* in pieces, prespeech, incoherent, silent, splayed, frightening. It was created on some border between domesticity and work, between action and inaction. Now that it's played out, there are only stills. Doors looking like dolmen. The roof was deep above you. Looking from windows when walls no longer exist is first silly then scary. A ladder is always only part way up, implying the rest. There is cartography in plaster walls, continents mapped for the first time. Rhythm and repetition of floor studs resemble bones of the rib cage. Finally, how calm is an open door left standing?

Day 8

Day 9, installation at the Willis Art Gallery

editing detroit

Detroit, Michigan, 1991
With Jean-Claude Azar, Jeanine Centuori,
Mary Douglas, Harah Frost, Jesse Goode,
Martin Tite, Simon Ungers, Michael Williams

We invited a group of artists, architects, and writers to remap the city of Detroit. A folded map of Detroit was drilled four times with a 3/4" hole saw. When unfolded, these holes formed a randomly generated grid of deleted areas. The participants then attempted to reestablish these lost areas in a variety of ways, which collectively formed a new map of Detroit.

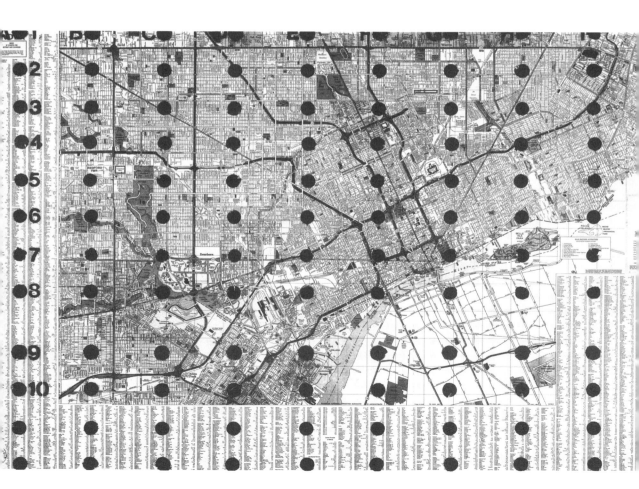

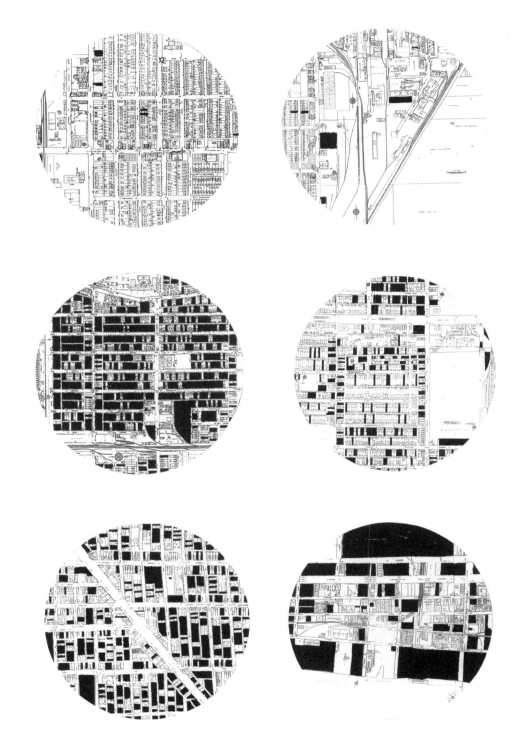

Blackened areas show demolition in the city from 1958 to 1988
Samples taken from downtown toward the suburbs, locations G2–G7

Editing Detroit

Terence Van Elslander

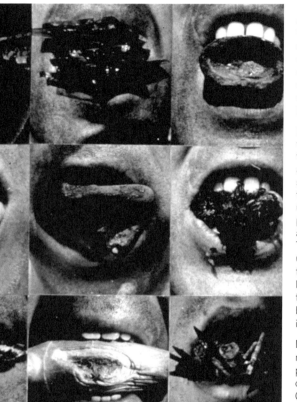

Detroit samples

Detroit is the city dedicated to mobility where everything has stopped. It is the most advanced city in the United States, in the sense that it has least resisted the demands of capital and consumption. White flight, expansion of the suburb, neighborhood destruction by freeway construction, the decay of building stock, racial strife, disinvestment, and unemployment have all been thoroughly explored in Detroit, where the politics of things have been brought about by the laws of profit.

Detroit is a city of complicity. What do architects think in a city with twelve thousand abandoned buildings? Architects helped to accomplish the ruin of Detroit. They were the technicians of a massive demolition, masquerading as urban renewal that only served to radically redistribute wealth. Architects serve power; they sublimate the crisis of necessity with the projection of utopian schemes and visions. Architects have been eager to provide persuasive forms to promote the destruction of polity and the erection of instruments of economic control. Why not? That is where the money is. Everyone else helped also: the unions, the hospitals, the blacks, the whites, the car companies, the climate, HUD, the suburbs, the Japanese, the freeways, New York. In return for their diligence, architects were allowed to erect the temples of suburban life: the malls, the office buildings, and the acres of identical houses. Architecture illuminates Detroit.

Detroit is overcome with greed. Ford's genius was the mobilization of desire. His statement, "We will overcome the problems of the city by leaving it," is both prophecy and directive. No impediment to consumption is permissible. Consumption must be promoted as the ideology of the correct use of the city.

In the 1930s car companies began to exhaust the productive capacities of Detroit and started to move their capital and factories elsewhere. So too, advanced consumers left the city for the suburb. No group, no neighborhood, no place could resist the powerful will of the city to devour itself. As financial resources left the city, the struggle to exit became increasingly bitter. The system that had once made commodities plentiful now made work scarce.

Detroit is a city of future past. What could be more real than poverty, despair, and confinement in a decaying neighborhood in Detroit? The fact that many thousands live in such a situation is difficult to accept. How does one reconcile Detroit with America, the self-proclaimed land of the free and champion of democracy? The systematic consolidation of the urban waste across America is too painful to see clearly. Instead they erect a talisman, that peculiar American utopian vision, rooted in the past. We cover inconsistency. They take refuge in a nostalgic desire to resurrect a past that never was and to make that the future. It is possible the good old days in Detroit never were. Not if you were black, poor, and living two families to a slum shack. And maybe not if you were working-class white so fearful that you erected a concrete wall to keep blacks out. Utopia of the past, which informs American culture from Jefferson to Bush, functions in Detroit to make the city seen as it is not; rather, they only see Motown, the Arsenal of Freedom, the Renaissance City. They do not see the real Detroit.

Detroit is a city of fear. Fear is codified and maintained by the physical layout of the city, which organizes the population according to race and class. The freeway system, which divides the city into segments, isolates the city from the suburb and provides escape routes for commuters. Detroit has inverted the notion of the fortified city by keeping danger within its walls. Detroit has achieved a panoptic condition, where everyone is simultaneously surveyed and surveyor. Fear is a necessity. It maintains the isolation of the individual and thwarts cooperation. The example of poverty and violence, so clearly framed, is a warning to secure one's place on the ladder of consumption. Desire and scarcity will create demand. There is no rest in Detroit.

Opposing photographs using twelve-square-inch mirrors,
locations G5, G3, G7

Urban Center for Contemporary Arts,
Grand Rapids, Michigan, 1990

This installation took place in a building located beside an electrical substation. Our goal was to measure the exact amount of power available to the building. To this end, we connected a series of resistance wires to the gallery's ceiling grid. These wires glowed red hot when current passed through them. They were held from the ceiling to the floor with plastic bags filled with water, which maintained tension as the resistors contracted and expanded. During the installation, when each circuit reached its maximum load, we rerouted the remaining circuits to the gallery space until all available power was harnessed. The total resistance that the electrical system of this building could handle was 23.739 ohms.

Neighboring electrical substation

displacement

Carleton University, Ottawa, Canada, 1989

Brick arches were dismantled, moved, and stacked in a solid mass.

Existing arches

Cancelled:

"The project was not an object but an action. A prolonged meditation on the act of building."

—Martin Tite

Our goal in this project was to work with the school building as directly as possible. After our initial inspection of the school, what struck us as most problematic was the existence of a nonstructural but massive (16' x 10') set of brick arches, crammed between two structural columns. The building is a cast-in-place concrete structure, designed in the early seventies. When erected, the unauthorized arches created a furor in the institution; charges of dishonesty, disrespect, and absurdity were hurled in every direction. It seemed certain that the arches would be removed.

However, after more than a decade, the arches remained. It was clear to us that the arches imposed an arthritic condition on the thought of the school. Not only were the arches blocking what was originally a well-formed, well-lit space, but they were also blocking something else—or, rather, they supported something else. The arches had become symbols of tradition and craft, yet they were only substitutes.

Our proposal was simple. First we disengaged the material, the bricks, from their mythological duties by dismantling the arches. The bricks were cleaned and then re-formed into a mass measuring 4' 4" x 3' 8" x 8' high. This labor took three days.

The administration's first response was that of having been deceived. They felt that we had done nothing and that our work lacked significance. This was almost the case. By eliminating the mytho-poetic content of the arches, we had created a void. Our lack of willingness to signify, or to sanction signification in our work, offended the institution. They were horrified at the prospect of an unnameable and unconsumable work. We had evaporated a voluble myth and offered in its place a mute presence, which could not be reproduced or communicated.

The school cancelled the exhibition.

Demolition process

Displacements

Andrew Payne

"[To] regain pure language fully formed in the linguistic flux is the tremendous and only capacity of translation. In this pure language ... all communication, all sense, and all intention finally encounter a stratum in which they are destined to be extinguished."

—Walter Benjamin

Displacement, an early work by Cathcart, Fantauzzi, and Van Elslander[1] undertaken at Carleton University in 1989, captures in germinal form an attitude to materials and their potential for productive transformation that is sustained throughout all the projects presented here. In the interest of clarifying this attitude, let me begin by recalling a comment made by Martin Tite, an acquaintance of and sometime collaborator with C/F/V. Speaking of *Displacement,* Tite avers that "the project was not an object but an action." Whether unconsciously or by design, Tite's remark contests a distinction first enshrined by Aristotle in his *Nichomachean Ethics*, a distinction between *poeisis* and *praxis*: "for production (*poiesis*) has an end other than itself, but action (*praxis*) does not: good action is itself an end."[2]

Somewhat closer to us in time, Hannah Arendt places Aristotle's distinction between poeisis and praxis at the center of her eulogizing description of the Greek conception of political life. According to Arendt, the great fallacy of political modernity, be it in its liberal or its socialist forms, consists in a tendency to equivocate the difference between acting and making, an equivocation whose result is, on her argument, "[t]he instrumentalization of politics and the degradation of everyday life."[3] This classicizing conception of political life and the perils attendant on its modernization is openly hostile to the precepts of advanced political economy (which tend to reify the mortal fragility and contingency of action). It is also utterly silent concerning the most radical tendencies to be observed in the cultural and aesthetic avant-gardes whose emergence was contemporary with the ascendancy of that economy, tendencies in which the forms of production associated with the fine arts seemed to assume the status of virtual acts. More attuned than was Arendt to the political and aesthetic realities of our times, Giorgio Agamben identifies "gesture" (a communicative modality that in his vocabulary has no subjective implication) as an operation whose effect is to dissolve the classical distinction between making and action: "if producing is a means in view of an end and *praxis* is an end without means, the gesture ... presents ... means that, as such, evade the orbit of mediality without becoming, for this reason, ends.... The gesture is, in this sense, communication of a communicability."[4] How might this conception of gesture, with its "communication of a communicability," assist us in clarifying the peculiar equivocation of fabrication and action Tite observes in *Displacement*?

In considering this question, it is perhaps helpful to bear in mind that the term *communication* (from the Latin stem *communicat-*) originally referred not only to the transport of intellectual or spiritual properties, but also to the conveyance of their material counterparts. I point this out because frequently the operation at stake in C/F/V's work involves the translation of a material element (or aggregate of such elements) from one place and morphological disposition to another. *Displacement* is no exception; in this work a quantum of bricks is conveyed from a plastic organization echoing the Latinate inflection of the tectonic language of Greek column architecture, viz. three nonstructural arches, into a new and resolutely a-signifying, indeed entropic, plastic paradigm, viz. a 4' 4" x 3' 8" x 8' cube into which the bricks were subsequently recomposed. According to Van Elslander, this conveyance signals a refusal to make these materials and the formations to which they are susceptible the support for defunct cultural and aesthetic values. Speaking of the university's response to the work, he observes that "[the administration at Carleton University] felt that…our work lacked significance. This was almost the case. By eliminating the mytho-poetic content of the arches, we had created a void. Our lack of willingness to signify, or to sanction signification in our work, offended the institution." Perhaps, but according to a law whose inexorability gives to all being-in-the-world the fate of being-in-language, "this lack of willingness to signify" still signifies, if only its own aversion to signification. In doing so, it transforms the very lack whose nullity it would avow into a kind of quasi-substance. Put simply, in the absence of other, more positive content, the work comes to mean its refusal to mean. How to make this refusal legible is, if I am not mistaken, the special preoccupation of these works. We might describe them as the pursuit of mediation without end, at once a practice of referral that functions in the absence of any final referent and a practice of formation that persistently definalizes form.

Seen from the perspective of the constructive process itself, this pursuit is expressed as a tendency to imbue the finished product with something of the uncertainty and contingency of those practices that first brought it into being, to return to it something of the formal and semantic indeterminacy that marked the process of its construction. Here the assiduous inscription of traces indexing an earlier and unfinished state is as much proleptic as it is retrospective, for it carries an implication that incompletion is not merely the prehistory but also the eternally repeated destiny of all fabricated things.[5] It is from the perspective offered by that implication that C/F/V's emphasis on process and the temporality of performance finds its proper register. These works are hymns to morphological impermanence, to what the first martyr of modern thought, Giordano Bruno, described as the capacity of any one thing, given time, to turn into any other.

Completed project

Having said this, one must distinguish the ethos that informs this work from the celebrations of infinite plasticity that dominate architectural theory in its current state. Missing from this ethos are two fantasies fundamental to the latter: the first is the fantasy of a world that offers no resistance to the formalizing impulse, an immaterial world in a precisely Aristotelian sense; the second is the fantasy of an infinite prosthetic extension of the mortal body's animate capacities. Unlike the digital utopias lionized by Deleuze's architectural epigones, these projects transpire in meat time. The labor that brings them into being is undertaken at a scale commensurate with the human body and across durations commensurate with the temporality that this body, in its own mortal becoming, undergoes. The photographs that document this work are populated with such mortal bodies, solitary figures busy at the task of making and unmaking an obdurate world. Like the characters of Samuel Beckett (Van Elslander's favorite writer), these figures are at once singular and anonymous, tragic and comical. Let us say that they are the denizens of an utterly disenchanted planet, one in which what would remain of redemption must consist in surrendering constructive self-assertion to a gesture that gives play to a spontaneity immanent in matter itself.

There is one photograph of *Displacement* that especially stays with me. It shows a man kneeling in a pile of bricks, absorbed in the task of cleaning them. Gazing at this figure, I am reminded of those medieval monks who saw in manual labor a form of prayer. But to what or to whom might this figure be prayin, and for what? Let us imagine him praying to the world of objects made and unmade, praying that this world might appear to him, its lips parted not by the effort of speech, but by that effort's everlasting imminence—as though this world might indicate by that gesture the mystery that resides not in its heart but on its surfaces, its palpable lack of willingness to signify.

[1] Hereafter referred to as C/F/V.

[2] Aristotle, *Nichomachean Ethics*, trans. Martin Oswald (Indianapolis: Bobbs-Merrill Educational Publishing, 1977), 245.

[3] Hannah Arendt, *The Human Condition*, second ed. (Chicago: University of Chicago Press, 1998), 230.

[4] Giorgio Agamben, *Means Without End: Notes on Politics*, trans. Vincenzo Binetti and Cesare Casarino (Minnesota: University of Minnesota Press, 2000), 56.

[5] This concern to index the process of composition and subsequent decomposition of the object is apparent in the assiduous documentation of the work. However, it is also, on occasion, a dimension of the work itself, to the extent that it makes sense to speak of such a thing. Such is the case in *Treatment of Fractures*, *Slump*, *Auschwitz*, *Excavation*, and *Hive [Arch]*.

Solid brick mass

big orbits

Big Orbit Gallery, Buffalo, New York, 2000
In collaboration with Mehrdad Hadighi

Space is constructed by the body in motion. The exterior placement of an interior geometry. Forty-six hundred shipping palettes were stacked in a gallery space adjoining a courtyard of identical shape. Elliptical geometry was used to carve an ovoid volume from the palette stack. Simultaneously an ovoid solid was carved in the courtyard.

The work functions as a scale, balancing positive and negative, apogee and center. A lever of space.

Void in progress

Solid in progress

Completed solid

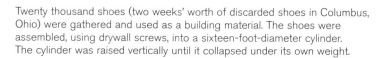

Hopkins Gallery, Ohio State University,
Columbus, Ohio, 1994

Twenty thousand shoes (two weeks' worth of discarded shoes in Columbus, Ohio) were gathered and used as a building material. The shoes were assembled, using drywall screws, into a sixteen-foot-diameter cylinder. The cylinder was raised vertically until it collapsed under its own weight.

Collapsed cylinder

Eight hundred bags of Quikrete were stacked like masonry over a thirty-five-foot-long bundle of dead trees, gathered from the nearby forest. The trees will rot away over time, leaving a freestanding arch of cured Quikrete bags.

New York, New York, 1996

Stopstopstopstopstop

Donald Kunze

Aposiopesis is the figure of speech that terminates speech, calling for the power of silence to replace the rattle of discourse from subject to subject and the correlative use of discourse as a "model" for "interrogating/valuing" the object. Far from being the justification for a negative response or a purism dedicated to the heroic material gestures of mute art, aposiopesis is the most eloquent of rhetorical tricks. By breaking off suddenly, a wave of feeling (let's call it pleasure-pain) rushes into the gulf created by the reversal of what is expected.

At the farewell concert of the famous Dutch soprano Elly Ameling, the singer began her final number, Schubert's *An die Musik*, itself filled with a restraint of feeling that could be counted as aposiopesis. But she broke off unexpectedly when the song "got to her," bringing the audience to an intensely painful moment of sadness, mixed with the inexplicable pleasure of being present at such a momentous occasion.

Another musical example demonstrates that silence can sometimes amount to reserve when expressiveness is expected. The pianist Dinu Lipati, suffering from an incurable disease and kept alive only through expensive treatments financed by his friends, decided to give a final concert for his benefactors before ceasing the treatments. He particularly avoided using pauses or dynamics that would stylistically represent the pathos of the moment, but the effect was devastating for the audience. The reserve and tranquility of the performance recalled the stoic last moments of the band playing on the deck of the Titanic, a moment that could be accused of being neither sentimental nor heroic in any way that would subsequently bleach out the pure *stain* left by combining horror with pleasure. Even on the recording of Lipati's concert, the effect can be heard and appreciated without knowing the circumstances.

Kent Kleinman has aptly remarked that work such as appears in this monograph should be "situated in practice, where it belongs." This is followed by an injunction *not to mention* Gordon Matta-Clark, Richard Serra, etc. that seems at first coy. Are these not the obvious precedents for projects that situate themselves at architecture's margins? The point, however, is not to characterize practice as a muscular, mute engagement of reality, in contrast to theory's pale reliance on ambiguous but sophisticated language, but rather to remind us that practice is, after all, closely related to *praxis*, the sum-total of all that can be known about human beings as social animals. Thus, we know more about music when we hear Ameling or Lipati break off or attenuate the music unexpectedly, than when we hear a complete, dutifully expressive performance.

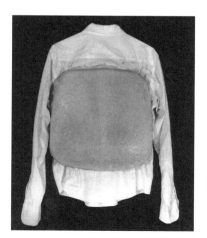

Resin relief, seat

Nonetheless, praxis would not be what it is—nor practice, nor human beings—were it not for language, which, by virtue of the duplicity of signs, forces us to live in two worlds at the same time. We pay attention to the network of symbolic relationships where conventions lubricate tenuous relationships with authority; but we also make fantasy projections of another subject who escapes this authority, a subject who is "supposed to know," a construct requiring us to imagine a point of view able to see through appearances, to penetrate the anamorphic blob that stains our view. *Theoria,* literally "bearing witness to the appearance of a god," is the access to the pleasure-pain that condenses the missing core that robs conventional meaning of any ultimate truth.

A work displayed in a museum or gallery interrupts us, commands us to be silent as an audience. Art historian Richard Bernheimer has noted that paintings that depict the rising of the soul from the tomb to heaven borrow from the imagery of the theater. Saints, cherubim, and the seraphic attendants of God take their place in concentric rows of seats like theater attendees. So silence is also structure. Our fantasy projection is also the impossible topology that connects final effects with origins and makes the effect into the cause.

Philosopher and critic Slavoj Zizek points to an example from Hitchcock's *Shadow of a Doubt.* The niece, Charlie, goes out on a date with a young FBI agent, who is tailing her suspicious uncle, also named Charlie. Charlie soon realizes that the real purpose of the date is to get her to reveal information about her uncle. Her horrified reaction to this realization abruptly breaks off the conversation. She responds not to the flirtatious conversation but, rather, snaps into the Real of the Real-ization that her uncle is being treated as a suspect in a murder investigation. In effect, the horrified look goes directly to the origin of the sequence that trips the murder investigation. It is not literally the cause of her uncle's string of homicides, but it does create *directly* the pleasure-pain that comes with the recognition of the "impossible" thesis. A god does rather literally appear: theory.

An idiotic symmetry pervades current theoretical discourse in architecture. Dominated by the "dialectic of presence and absence," which is easily converted into the currency of practice and theory, a conundrum of opposition leads to a debate about origins: does theory precede or follow practice? This is a question with no more or less sense to it than Vitruvius's account of the origin of architecture in the discovery of and subsequent adaptation to fire. *Post hoc ergo propter hoc* is a tempting fallacy, but effect often precedes cause where the trauma of teleology and its alloy of chance and necessity are concerned. Zizek tells a joke about the puzzled little girl who noted that "Daddy was born in Manchester, Mummy in Bristol and I in London: strange that the three of us should have met!" The suppressed element "returns" to frame the scene "from the inside," which is to say that human cause and logical cause are not always the same thing—particularly where fantasy is the only way to escape the catch-22 structure of reality.

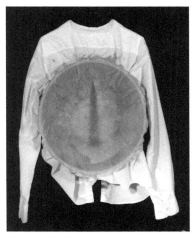

Resin relief, bowl

Resin relief, paint tray

Hitchcock knew this in other ways as well, especially in the physical structure of the set of *Rear Window*, where the bachelor-killer and the bachelor-pursuer meet through a suture of space familiar to all city dwellers, whose visual space is so differently structured from their pedestrian world. The flashbulb defense should be familiar to fans of the Homeric episode of the Cyclops, where a "poke in the eye with a burnt stick" now takes the illuminating form of a monocular blinding bulb, all to focus on the "nobody" who hounded the killer out of his lair— "her bachelors, even," as Duchamp would put it.

Krzysztof Kieslowsky's *Red* and David Lynch's *Mulholland Drive* are equally insistent on putting fantasy before fact, the Vichian True of the imagination before the Made of praxis. In *Red*, the judge "does not exist" except for Valentine, whose fatalistic-chiastic meeting with her future love, Auguste, depends on the behind-the-scenes manipulation of the retired jurist. *Mulholland Drive* counterpoints the fantasy of dead-dying Betty-Diane with the reality sequence where the producer, Adam, reluctantly casts and then marries Camilla Rhodes. Diane "does not exist," is repressed, and returns as the ingénue Betty. Her resurrection ("Time to wake up, pretty girl," says the mysterious cowboy) in time to answer the phone invitation, takes us back to the primal scene, the limousine driving slowly along Mulholland Drive.

The moments of these films are like the one in *The Sixth Sense*, when the psychiatrist realizes that he is one of the dead people his psychotic young patient sees and the audience realizes in retrospect that, like the judge in *Red*, it has not really seen him interact with anyone other than the point-of-view character. It is a moment that "returns the repressed" with a force of realization and emotion. It returns to a place *emptied out* by the Other, made vacant, void, meaningless through an act of clearing, negation, or cutting off—all tricks of aposiopesis.

Mulholland Drive shares an important feature with thriller writer Stephen King's *Pet Cemetery*. The desire to bring a loved pet or loved child back to life is the half-life of the zombie returned from the grave, the corpse, unsuccessfully laid to rest, who is between "two deaths" and "doesn't know it's dead yet." Is not the audience precisely the kind of being who "doesn't know it's dead yet," who is "between the two deaths," the first death endured upon entering the theater, the second upon the final reception of the *idea* of the work of art? At least, if Bernheimer is right, they're sitting in the right place.

So architecture made into spectacle is not such a bad idea, particularly if it rescues theory from the presence-absence conundrum that forces it out of language—when in fact language itself would force it out of language through the device of aposiopesis; when in fact the sign would force it into metonymy even if metaphor should be imposed on it through the question of origins or the crisis of interpretation.

Let us not speak, then, of Gordon Matta-Clarke or Richard Serra, or others on Kleinman's list, if only out of respect for the muteness and eloquence of those aposiopetic performances and ones that have continued their dark vision. The ambiguity of death, which leads children to bury birds and other found animals with ritual refinements befitting the Druids, is the same ambiguity of silence that leads us to the sense of decorum where new meaning is born (*hapax*) out of the carcass of the returned zombie in funeral garb. Surplus = lack; effect = cause; pleasure = pain. Such is life, or, rather, death-in-life. No surprise that Dracula was strangely sexy.

These inversions would be surprising were they not so plentiful. Maya Lin's lucky experiment with reflections led to one of the most successful architectural uses of suture and silence, the Vietnam Veterans Memorial in Washington, D.C., where visitors get to exchange gifts and messages with the spectral dead, animated by their own mirror images. Luck is more often the stuff of history rather than art. An even more compelling, and simultaneously more subtle, memorial to a trauma of the past is the permanently unused gate to the Technical University of Athens, an entry closed off since tanks stormed it during the junta of the generals in the 1960s.

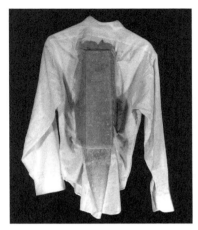

Resin relief, anvil

What's to see when we look into or *with* the eyes of the dead? The absence or negation of something familiar: the recollection that the psychiatrist has not talked to any living person (*The Sixth Sense*); the ring belonging to a murdered woman (*Shadow of a Doubt*); the ring without its owner (*Rear Window*); the rotting corpse, Diane (*Mulholland Drive*); the house lying in pieces (*Azar, Cathcart, Fantauzzi, Van Elslander, Williams*); the honey pump lying on the floor of the Louisiana Museum in Denmark (*Beuys*); the restrained performance of Lipati or the missing verses of *An die Musik*.

These are a few of my favorite things.

But, unlike the Rogers and Hammerstein raindrops-on-roses list, these are uncanny Gahen Wilson mementos that operate like Lacanian *sinthoms*, voids of meaning around which actions spiral as they do around Dante's frustrated lovers, Paulo and Francesca. What does the architect bring to these things/moments/*mementi*?

Italo Calvino's answers for literature serve architecture even better: lightness and heaviness, quickness and slowness; visibility and invisibility (the "phallic" qualities of architecture), exactitude, multiplicity, and finally consistency, which is best evidenced when, in the face of human limitations, it just has to stop.

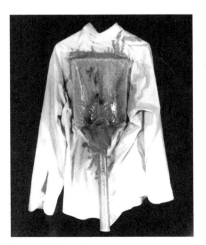

Resin relief, shovel

Cranbrook Academy of Art, Bloomfield Hills, Michigan, 1992
With John Wright, Sean Murphy

A single parking space in a parking lot was excavated eight feet deep. A van was lowered into the hole and cast in concrete. The van was then excavated to reveal its cast.

Earthworm Casts

Tod Williams

When I think of casts and muse far beyond the standard materials of molten metal, concrete, and plaster, I eventually enter the world of worms and earthworm casts. I associate them with childhood memories of fishing, walks in the woods, and excavations for new houses. I am crouched down, staring at the tiny mountains of earthworm casts, and I try to visualize the earth below, the world beneath my feet. There are worms penetrating the packed muddy floor and, once below, alongside them thousands of ants working furiously, creating tunnels, moving and removing granules, passing food through seemingly infinite passageways, carving a life underground.

I have often been asked how I can bear to wait the three to four years it takes to bring a building to reality. My response is that I am happy to design a building that will be built. If I have my way, it could take longer, for not only do I take pleasure in the process, but I can continue to improve the design. Long nights in the studio made me realize as a student that this was a life I could live. It is not glamorous, as portrayed; rather, it has something to do with that never ending world of worms and ants. We always seem to be working.

> The work is about doing.... The work is from the inside. The work is about no thing. The work is about section.... We want insight. We want ideation. We want less.... We want to open the foundation. We want the joints.... We want to assemble facts. We want silence.
>
> —Cathcart, Fantauzzi, Van Elslander, 2002

I first encountered this work at the Cranbrook Academy of Art in the summer of 1992, during the ACSA summer workshop. Over the course of three days they dug a very large hole in a parking lot, inverted a van, and placed it upside down in the hole. Removing the innards of the van, much the way the creatures of the earth remove flesh from a corpse, they then poured concrete into the space between the van and the earth. Once hardened, the shell of the van was removed, leaving the interior form of the van in the ground. It was an amazing sight, and it revised the way I understood the van, the land, and, perhaps, architecture.

It was not lost on me that the clumsy gas-guzzling van was a product of Detroit. Furthermore, many of us remember that this very parking lot had obliterated the academy's tennis courts. Today the studio building for metals and ceramics, designed by Raphael Moneo, sits on the exact site of *Excavation*. The sheer physical effort required to accomplish the project mandated complete devotion by those working on the excavation. They were, thus, unavailable to visit the rest of the campus or participate in the symposia. They were just hardworking people in a big hole in the parking lot, fully invested in Cranbrook's true mission: the interconnection of landscape, art, and architecture through craft. The *Excavation* project perfectly addressed something that is quintessential to an architectural education: revelation through immersion.

Concrete cast after excavation

Storefront for Art and Architecture, New York, New York, 1996
With Jared Handelsman

One hundred fifteen discarded objects were collected from the streets of downtown Manhattan; Williamsburg, Brooklyn; and Long Island City, Queens.

A self-supporting structure, spanning the interior columns was built with these objects wrapped in industrial Saran Wrap as a tensile exterior skin.

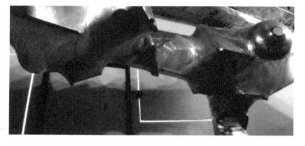

Sample of objects

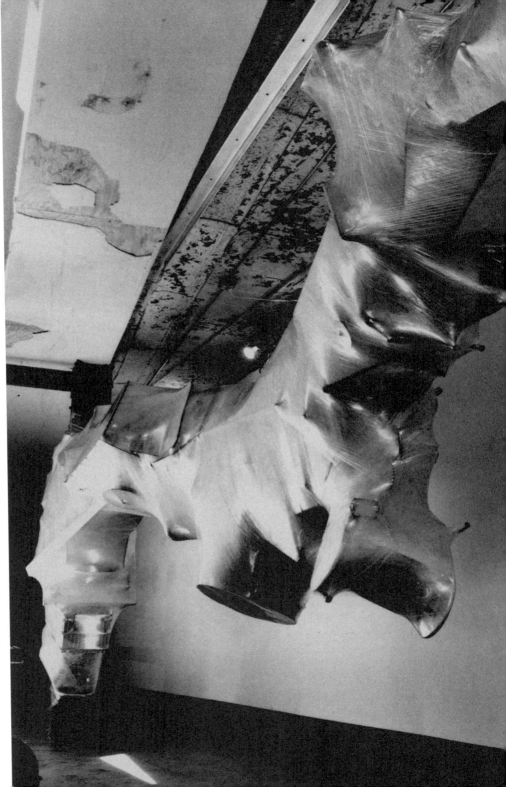

Gallery interior

Carleton University, Ottawa, Canada, 1995

Installation using industrial-strength Saran Wrap and office chairs to span two structural columns. Though nothing else attached the chairs but the wrapping material in tension, the completed arch was strong enough to support a person.

Wrapped chairs around a column
Capp Street Project,
San Francisco, California, 1995

Completed arch

Hallwalls Contemporary Arts Center, Buffalo, New York, 2001
With Anthony Dong

In an eighty-year-old concrete building, one hundred gallons of latex were painstakingly, obsessively painted onto a twenty-six-hundred-square-foot concrete floor. In one section inflation valves, cut from bicycle inner tubes, were layered into the coats. In another section a two-by-four-inch steel beam, lift hooks attached, was immured in the seventeen coats of latex. When dry, the valves were inflated and the beam was ratcheted toward the ceiling.

Suck and Blow

Philip Beesley

Latex on plywood models

The first thing is the smell of ammonia. The atmosphere leeches from the four hundred liters of latex rubber layered over the eighty-year-old concrete floors of the warehouse building. It surrounds you and gives a faint bite as you breathe. The acrid scent you find inside leaves the question of its origin. Disease? Instincts waver, guarded.

The two spaces of the project have been coated to their outer limits with multiple layers, translucent and mottled. One space has taut metal cables hanging from the center of the ceiling and attached to a spine set inside the rubber skin on the floor. As the cables pull up the spine, the latex skin lifts with it, forming a long, upside-down hull. The thick elastic walls curve inward up to the spine and suck hard at the floor. The air around pushes back down on this void, collapsing the surfaces inward.

The latex sticks very slightly to the touch. As you pull your hand away, it gives a faint, unpeeling tug. If you recoil, it follows you for an instant. The latex skin rebounds away, and a tiny quiver telegraphs into the hollow belly of the vessel.

The second space is filled by an opposite twin, an immense air-filled blister, breaking outward from the rubber skin of the floor and rising up to head height. An inner-tube valve that declares the method of inflation marks this obese curve. A rectangular slip sheet set under the center of each lamination breaks the bond between the rubber and the floor slab to make these voids. Instant rooms.

The title *Push/Pull* sounds like a simple play. By operating primary forces against each other, you build a new balanced constant, a kind of gravity. Outward and inward. The play of forces against the floor and ceiling is strong. This is a little theater of robust forces, where pure equations of matter can be enjoyed. And, for a while, the construction seems elegant, tidy.

Push, painted floor

Pull, painted floor

Pull, detail

But why is the form bulging? Blisters do that—more glimmers of revulsion. Then the outer skins of the two rooms are underfoot. The skins are continuous with the floor, molding to your shoes and planting you. The friction is surprisingly aggressive.

The first steps on this surface were a pleasure, firmly planted location salving the slightly tensed posture that comes inevitably from living on hollow city slabs. But this ground is not there to serve as firm foundation. Pressing down with the weight of your body into the multiple laminations, you feel the rubber react like the flesh of a succulent, letting you in, first softly and then with a hunger closing on the soles of your feet. The looming pair puff and suck and bloat, bulging. They have you in their sticky skirts. Blowup love dolls writ large feel *me*.

Pull

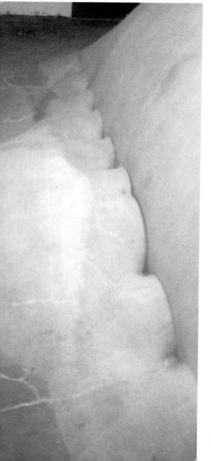

The experience is ambivalent to its core. Methodical actions of pushing and pulling and layering of material define this work. Measures of orientation and substance accumulate here—achieved by concentration and repetition—while at the same time the world of these instant rooms is tinged with loss: nearly warm, nearly a greeting. Part of it is confident. To the nineteenth-century German art theorist Robert Vischer, this kind of experience was an act of grace:

> Thus I project my own life into the lifeless form…a secret, scarcely suppressed twitching of the limbs, a timorous yearning, a gesturing and a stammering…accompanied by a concrete emotional element of feeling that is inseparably bound up with the concept of human wholeness.[1]

And mixed with that confidence, yawning beneath this new locus of dense gravity, is abjection. Theorist Julia Kristeva dwells, like Cathcart, Fantauzzi, and Van Elslander, in her *Powers of Horror*, "neither jovial, nor trustful, nor sublime, nor enraptured by preexisting harmony. It is bare…pitted with blank spaces where emotion does not allow itself to be dolled up in flower sentences."[2]

The empathy that Cathcart, Fantauzzi, and Van Elslander offer is unrelieved by any reliable sense of wholeness. A poignant kind of laughter, then. My daughter deliberately spins to taste dizziness, and *Push/Pull* works to create substance out of a void. They are not so different. The vertigo that *Push/Pull* gives is tinged dark, because the firm ground secured by natural gravity has been lost. It holds only a little optimism, but it seems cousin still to Robert Vischer's "empathy." He says that when we encounter work like this, "the whole person and all his vital feeling are lured into compassion."[3]

Push/Pull: a mechanical empathy. New gravity.

[1] Robert Vischer, "On the Optical Sense of Form: A Contribution to Aesthetics," *Empathy, Form and Space: Problems in German Aesthetics, 1873–1893* (Santa Monica: Getty Center, 1994), 104.

[2] Julia Kristeva, *Powers of Horror*, trans. Leon S. Roudiez (New York: Columbia University Press, 1982), 208–9.

[3] Vischer, "On the Optical Sense of Form," 107.

Push, detail

Push

Capp Street Gallery, San Francisco, California, 1995

Sixty tons of recycled paper were bought at market price, warehoused in the gallery for the duration of the installation, then sold at market price.

Gallery interior

Paper

Recycled paper is one of San Francisco's largest businesses. The paper market prices fluctuate seasonally, not unlike the stock market.

The project became a venue to address the following discourse: is a gallery essentially a warehouse, which by its nature treats art like any other commodity, with price fluctuations affected directly by the art market? Does the price of a work of art increase in value by the fact that it is being warehoused in a higher-rent environment? Is a work validated as art by being warehoused in the gallery context? Can one hold onto an "art stock" for the duration of an exhibition, then sell it at a higher price? Is the recycled-paper effort in our "paperless society" just another high-profit business in eco-utopian disguise?

Sixty tons of purchased recycled paper arrived in bails in two eighteen-wheelers. The forklift operator, given full freedom to place the bails as he pleased, stacked them against the corner to provide the forklift with the optimal turning radius. Behind the gallery's glass facade, the shredded paper formed a solid mass.

We should have turned a profit by storing the paper until there was a rise in the market price. Halfway through the course of the exhibition the San Francisco Fire Department forced an early sale, and no profit was made.

Buy low. Sell high.

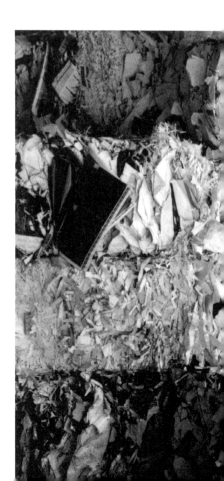

artist residency: artists invited to live and work

at Capp Street Project during which they create

a new work for exhibition

exhibition progr

throughout the ye

national and inte

esentations scheduled

new works by regional,

al contemporary artists

installation art: an art form that has

boundaries but is an environment cr

specific site

Storefront for Art and Architecture, New York, New York, 1992

With a budget of five hundred dollars, five portable construction toilets were rented and inserted into the facade of the Storefront for Art and Architecture, in New York, left open to the public, and serviced for six weeks.

Storefront, February 1, 1992

Storefront, February 8, 1992

During installation

Gallery exterior

Gallery interior

Gravity

This work is about seeing

This work is about doing

This work is about opening

This work is about touch

This work is about tools

This work is from the inside

This work is about no thing

This work is section

Not a project, a utopia of form, a hope, an image

Not an argument, a goal, a directive

Not a commission

Not subject

Not beauty, angles, shape

Not design

Not compensation

Not solution

We want insight

We want ideation

We want less

We want the joints

We want to open the foundation

We want to assemble facts

We want silence

About the Authors:

James Cathcart, Frank Fantauzzi, and Terence Van Elslander have been collaborating since 1988. They are the founders of icebergproject.org. Their work has been exhibited and published widely in North America and Europe.

James Cathcart is from Colombia. He completed his master's degree in architecture at the Cranbrook Academy of Art and has worked extensively in North and South America, Asia, and Europe. He lives in New York City.

Frank Fantauzzi is from Italy. He is an associate professor of architecture at the University at Buffalo. He completed his professional studies at Carleton University in Canada and his postprofessional studies at the Cranbrook Academy of Art. His work engages critical forms of architectural practice.

Terence Van Elslander is from Canada. He is an architect in Toronto and an adjunct assistant professor at the University of Toronto. He received his professional degree from Carleton University in Canada and his master of architecture from the Cranbrook Academy of Art.

About the Contributors:

Juhani Pallasmaa has held the positions of professor and dean at the Helsinki University of Technology (1991–97), the director of the Museum of Finnish Architecture, Helsinki (1978–83), and rector of the Institute of Industrial Design, Helsinki (1970–72). He has taught and lectured extensively in Europe, Africa, and North and South America, published books and exhibition catalogs, and contributed to a number of books and journals in twenty countries. His latest books are *Juhani Pallasmaa—Sensuous Minimalism* (Beijing, 2002), *The Architecture of Image: Existential Space in Cinema* (Helsinki, 2001), and *Alvar Aalto: Villa Mairea 1938–39* (Helsinki, 1998). He has directed his architectural office in Helsinki since 1983.

Kent Kleinman is an architect and professor of architecture, and chair of the Department of Architecture at the University at Buffalo. His work focuses on architecture, design, and design theory, and he has authored a number of books and articles on twentieth-century architecture.

Harah Frost is a writer, living in Detroit.

Andrew Payne is an assistant professor of history and theory in the Faculty of Architecture, Landscape, and Design at the University of Toronto. He has published writing on art, literature, politics, and architecture. He has also recently completed a doctoral dissertation on post-Romantic interpretations of Shakespeare's *Hamlet* in the Department of English at the University of Toronto and is currently working on a book on that topic.

Donald Kunze has taught architecture and general arts at Pennsylvania State University since 1984. He is the author of *Thought and Place*, on the philosophy of Giambattista Vico, as well as a book, in progress, on the boundaries of the mystery story and articles on the relationships of architecture and the arts to philosophy, topology, and culture. His latest work focuses on boundaries, recursion, and self-similar forms in the imagination of architectural and civic structures. He lives with his wife and three cats in Boalsburg, Pennsylvania.

Tod Williams, FAIA, FAAR, has been the principal of his own firm for the last twenty-eight years. The partnership of Tod Williams, Billie Tsien, and Associates was formed in 1986. This studio of fifteen people is well known for its wide range of projects, its exceptionally high standards, and work that emphasizes the importance of place and the exploration of the nature of materials. His built works include Feinberg Hall at Princeton University; Hereford College at the University of Virginia; Phoenix Art Museum addition and renovation; the Neurosciences Institute in La Jolla, California; Natatorium at the Cranbrook Schools in Michigan; Mattin Student Arts Center at Johns Hopkins University; and the American Folk Art Museum in New York City. Williams has been a teacher for more than thirty years. In 2002 he held the Eliel Saarinen chair at the University of Michigan. He presently holds the Louis I. Kahn chair at Yale University.

Philip Beesley is an architect and sculptor, working in Toronto and Waterloo, Ontario. He studies empathy and dissociation. His built works include public buildings, architectural textiles, and immersive environments.

Acknowledgments:

We dedicate this publication to our children, Paco Cathcart, Emilia and Saija Fantauzzi, and Eero Van Elslander.

We would like to acknowledge Anthony Dong for his profound contribution to the iceberg project and this publication. His commitment and understanding have made this project possible. We would like to thank Juhani Pallasma, Kent Kleinman, Harah Frost, Andrew Payne, Donald Kunze, Tod Williams, and Phillip Beesley for their written contribution and support; and our editor, Linda Lee. We would also like to thank Jean-Claude Azar, Michael Williams, Bill Cathcart, and the many friends, colleagues, and students who have contributed over the years. Our special thanks to Margaret Fantauzzi, Laura Stasior, and Sandra Van Elslander.

Project Credits:

Table of contents (p. 3); photos by Anthony Dong

Wall Hung, Brooklyn, New York, 1992 (p. 4), with Christopher Borrok, Michael Sedlacek

Still (p. 8), with Jeanine Centuori, Robert Crise, Francis Resendes; reconstruction and sequence photos by Francis Resendes

Slice [Still 1999] (pp. 9–15), with David Zielinski, Anthony Dong, Mehrdad Hadighi, Matthew Mancuso, Kerron Miller, Giona Paolercio, Shahin Vassigh, David Willard; photos by David Zielinski, Thomas Pederson, Cathcart/Fantauzzi/Van Elslander

Car Spin (pp. 16–17), with Tim Mizicko, Sean Murphy, Will Stanforth, Joseph Plenzler; photos by Will Stanforth, Frank Fantauzzi

9119 St. Cyril Street (pp. 18–23), with Jean-Claude Azar, Michael Williams; photos by Michael Williams, Cathcart/Fantauzzi/Van Elslander

Editing Detroit (pp. 24–29), with Jean-Claude Azar, Jeanine Centuori, Mary Douglas, Harah Frost, Jesse Goode, Martin Tite, Simon Ungers, Michael Williams

Big Orbits (pp. 38–41), in collaboration with Mehrdad Hadighi, assisted by Anthony Dong, Noburo Inoue, David Misenheimer, Nicholas Cameron, Melisa Delaney, Karen Li, Ted Lutz, Kerron Miller, Chris Paa, Mike Singh, Queenie Tong; photos by David Misenheimer, Frank Fantauzzi

Slump (pp. 42–43), with Dane Brubaker, Margaret Fantauzzi, Darren Kelly, John Wright, Michael Williams, Ruth King, Joe Volpe, Ellen Grevey, Prudence Gill

Hive (pp. 44–47), in collaboration with Anthony Dong, assisted by Joseph Chiafari, John Manhardt, David Mason, Jonathan Rule, Queenie Tong, David Zielinski; photos by Anthony Dong, Cathcart/Fantauzzi/Van Elslander

Excavation (pp. 52–55), with John Wright, Sean Murphy, John Bass, Rudolph Burton, Melisa Ficociello, Jose Garcia, Gian Luigi Mondaini, Richard Mohler, Dan Powers, Steven Stanley, Peter Wiederspahn; photos by Frank Fantauzzi, John Wright

Catenary (pp. 56–57), with Jared Handelsman; photos by James Cathcart, Jared Handelsman

Arch (pp. 58–59), thanks to Mark West

Push/Pull (pp. 60–67), with Anthony Dong; photos by Anthony Dong, Cathcart/Fantauzzi/Van Elslander

Car Props, Brooklyn, New York, 1990 (pp. 76–77)

Drilled NYC Subway Map, Brooklyn, New York, 1989 (p. 80)

Cover photo, interior of *Pull* project, *Push/Pull*

All photos and texts by Cathcart/Fantauzzi/Van Elslander, except where otherwise noted

In memory of

Ronald Petersen, 1960–2002